Our Holidays

Celebrate Memorial Day

Amy Hayes

Cavendish Square
New York

Published in 2015 by Cavendish Square Publishing, LLC
243 5th Avenue, Suite 136, New York, NY 10016

Copyright © 2015 by Cavendish Square Publishing, LLC

First Edition

Website: cavendishsq.com

This publication represents the opinions and views of the author based on his or her personal experience, knowledge, and research. The information in this book serves as a general guide only. The author and publisher have used their best efforts in preparing this book and disclaim liability rising directly or indirectly from the use and application of this book.

CPSIA Compliance Information: Batch #WW15CSQ

All websites were available and accurate when this book was sent to press.

Library of Congress Cataloging-in-Publication Data

Hayes, Amy.
Celebrate Memorial Day / Amy Hayes.
pages cm. — (Our holidays)
Includes index.
ISBN 978-1-50260-245-9 (hardcover) ISBN 978-1-50260-235-0 (paperback) ISBN 978-1-50260-240-4 (ebook)
1. Memorial Day—Juvenile literature. I. Title.

E642.H415 2015
394.262—dc23

2014032631

Senior Copy Editor: Wendy A. Reynolds
Art Director: Jeffrey Talbot
Designer: Joseph Macri
Senior Production Manager: Jennifer Ryder-Talbot
Production Editor: David McNamara
Photo Researcher: J8 Media

The photographs in this book are used by permission and through the courtesy of:
Cover photo by Robert D. Barnes/Moment Open/Getty Images; Daniel Bendjy/E+/Getty Images, 5;
U.S. Navy Petty Officer 3rd Class William Selby/File:Defense.gov photo essay 110917-N-5145S-005.jpg/Wikimedia Commons, 7; ©iStockphoto.com/Catherine Lane, 9;
PAUL J. RICHARDS/AFP/Getty Images, 11; STEPHEN D. CANNERELLI/The Post-Standard/Landov, 13; ©iStockphoto.com/Kali Nine LLC, 15;
©iStockphoto.com/Christopher Futcher, 17; Anatoliy Samara/iStock/Thinkstock, 19; Visual Ideas/Camilo Morales/Blend Images/Getty Images, 21.

Printed in the United States of America

Contents

Today is Memorial Day!

Memorial Day is the day we remember the **soldiers** who died **protecting** our country.

Memorial Day is held on the last Monday in May.

Today is the last Monday in May.

MAY

Sunday	Monday	Tuesday	Wednesday	Thursday	Friday	Saturday
					1	2
3	4	5	6	7	8	9
10	11	12	13	14	15	16
17	18	19	20	21	22	23
24	25	26	27	28	29	30
31						

9

We go to **memorials** and put flags on graves.

We listen to stories about the soldiers.

Then we go to a **parade**.

The parade celebrates
the soldiers.

13

After the parade, we have a **picnic**.

We grill hot dogs, hamburgers, and ears of corn.

It smells really good!

At the picnic, we play outside with our friends.

It's time to eat!

Happy Memorial Day!

20

21

New Words

memorials (me-MOR-ee-alz) Spaces and markers created to honor people who have died.

parade (pu-RAID) A public celebration, usually with many people in the street.

picnic (PIK-nik) A party that includes a meal eaten outdoors.

protecting (pro-TEK-ting) Keep something safe.

soldiers (SOL-jerz) People in military service.

Index

23

About the Author

Amy Hayes lives in the beautiful city of Buffalo. She celebrates Memorial Day by having cookouts with her family.

About BOOKWORMS

Bookworms help independent readers gain reading confidence through high-frequency words, simple sentences, and strong picture/text support. Each book explores a concept that helps children relate what they read to the world they live in.